anxiety relief

COLORING BOOK FOR TEENS

Creativity to Find Calm

CALLISTO PUBLISHING

Copyright © 2022 by Callisto Publishing LLC
Cover and internal design © 2022 by Callisto Publishing LLC
Illustrations © 2021 Collaborate Agency
Art Director: Patricia Fabricant
Art Producer: Hannah Dickerson
Editor: Elizabeth Baird
Production Editor: Jael Fogle
Production Manager: David Zapanta

Callisto Publishing and the colophon are registered trademarks of Callisto Publishing LLC

Published by Callisto Publishing LLC C/O Sourcebooks LLC
P.O. Box 4410, Naperville, Illinois 60567-4410
(630) 961-3900
callistopublishing.com

Printed and bound in China.
WKT 24

This Book Belongs to:

....

introduction

welcome to your anxiety relief coloring book!

The goal of this coloring book is to help you relax and celebrate your own unique style of creative expression. Studies show that the structured, focused, and artistic act of coloring reduces stress and quiets the mind, giving your brain a chance to rest. The great news: This helps relieve anxiety!*

The images in this book have been chosen to promote a sense of positivity, happiness, and serenity. As you clear your mind and use your artistic instruments of choice, be as creative as you like! Whether you've colored inside the lines or gone wild, what's important is that you've taken the time to invest in your well-being.

There's no wrong way to use this book. With 35 illustrations ranging from simple to complex, there's a page for all occasions. Flip to a page that looks fun to you, and use your colored pencils, fine-tipped markers, gel pens, or other chosen art supplies. Keep the pages for yourself or share them with friends—it's up to you. Happy coloring!

*If you have serious or ongoing anxiety, be sure to talk to a trusted adult or medical professional—it's always great to ask for help!

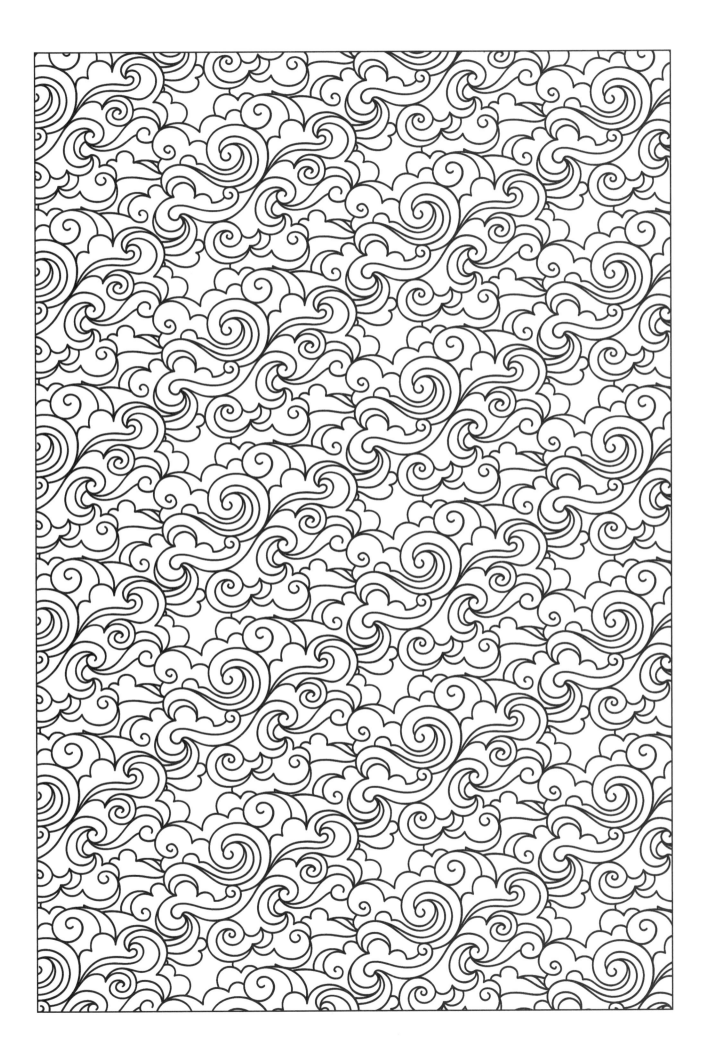